MW00680007

Discover
JOHN
THE LAMB OF GOD

by
Brent and Diane Averill

FAITH
ALIVE®
Christian Resources

Grand Rapids, Michigan

Cover photo: Corbis

The authors wish to acknowledge with thanks that in preparing their manuscript for this study they drew on some ideas for discussion questions and responses from two earlier studies produced in the Discover Your Bible series: *Discover Jesus in John: Who He Is* (1992) and *Discover Jesus in John: Why He Came* (1993) by Sylvia Boomsma. All rights reserved by Faith Alive Christian Resources.

We welcome your comments. Call us at 1-800-333-8300 or e-mail us at editors@faithaliveresources.org.

ISBN 978-1-59255-225-2

10 9 8 7 6 5 4 3 2

Contents

How to Study

The questions in this study booklet will help you discover what the Bible says. This is inductive Bible study—in which you will discover the message for yourself.

Questions are the key to inductive Bible study. Through questions you search for the writers' thoughts and ideas. The questions in this booklet are designed to help you in your quest for answers. You can and should ask your own questions too. The Bible comes alive with meaning for many people as they discover the exciting truths it contains. Our hope and prayer is that this booklet will help the Bible come alive for you.

The questions in this study are designed to be used with the New International Version of the Bible, but other translations can also be used.

Step 1. Read each Bible passage several times. Allow the ideas to sink in. Think about their meaning. Ask questions about the passage.

Step 2. Answer the questions, drawing your answers from the passage. Remember that the purpose of the study is to discover what the Bible says. Write your answers in your own words. If you use Bible study aids such as commentaries or Bible handbooks, do so only after completing your own personal study.

Step 3. Apply the Bible's message to your own life. Ask,

- What is this passage saying to me?
- How does it challenge me? Comfort me? Encourage me?
- Is there a promise I should claim? A warning I should heed?
- For what can I give thanks?

If you sense God speaking to you in some way, respond to God in a personal prayer.

Step 4. Share your thoughts with someone else if possible. This will be easiest if you are part of a Bible study group that meets regularly to share discoveries and discuss questions.

If you would like to learn of a study group in your area or would like information on training to start a small group Bible study,

- call toll-free 1-888-644-0814, e-mail smallgroups@crcna.org, or visit www.FaithAliveResources.org/DYB.

Introduction

The last days of Jesus' life have inspired countless books, movies, and musical pieces, and students of the Bible quickly discover that the events of those days fill the entire second half of the book of John. Shortly after raising his friend Lazarus from the dead at Bethany (John 11), Jesus rides into Jerusalem as the promised Son of David, the Messiah, the Son of God (John 12)—setting in motion an amazing week of events that complete his mission to save us from sin and death forever.

The gospel ("good news") message is true! Jesus Christ is "the Lamb of God, who takes away the sin of the world" (John 1:29). He became the ultimate sacrifice for sin by dying on a cross for our sake, and he conquered death and rose to life again so that "whoever believes in him shall not perish but have eternal life" (3:16).

As this study continues into the second half of the gospel account written by John, we pray that it may draw you closer to the one and only Savior, the eternal Son of God who "became flesh" to show us "the full extent of his love" (1:14; 13:1).

Jesus' Ministry

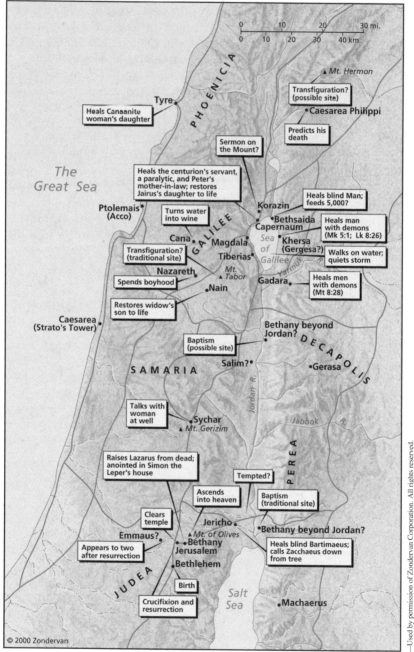

Heals Canaanite woman's daughter

Transfiguration? (possible site)

Caesarea Philippi

Predicts his death

Sermon on the Mount?

Heals the centurion's servant, a paralytic, and Peter's mother-in-law; restores Jairus's daughter to life

Heals blind Man; feeds 5,000?

Turns water into wine

Heals man with demons (Mk 5:1; Lk 8:26)

Transfiguration? (traditional site)

Walks on water; quiets storm

Spends boyhood

Heals men with demons (Mt 8:28)

Restores widow's son to life

Baptism (possible site)

Talks with woman at well

Raises Lazarus from dead; anointed in Simon the Leper's house

Tempted?

Ascends into heaven

Baptism (traditional site)

Clears temple

Appears to two after resurrection

Heals blind Bartimaeus; calls Zacchaeus down from tree

Birth

Crucifixion and resurrection

PHOENICIA

▲ Mt. Hermon

Tyre

The Great Sea

Ptolemais (Acco)

Korazin

Bethsaida

Capernaum

GALILEE

Cana

Magdala

Sea of Galilee

Khersa (Gergesa?)

Tiberias

Nazareth

Mt. Tabor

Gadara

Nain

Yarmuk

Caesarea (Strato's Tower)

Bethany beyond Jordan?

DECAPOLIS

SAMARIA

Salim?

Gerasa

Jordan R.

Sychar

▲ Mt. Gerizim

Jabbok R.

PEREA

Emmaus?

Jericho

▲ Mt. of Olives

Bethany

Jerusalem

Bethlehem

Bethany beyond Jordan?

JUDEA

Salt Sea

Machaerus

0 10 20 30 mi.
0 10 20 30 40 km.

© 2000 Zondervan

Glossary of Terms

Abraham—the father of the Israelite nation whom God called to follow him in faith. God also promised to bless "all peoples on earth" through Abraham (Gen. 12:3). Jesus ultimately fulfilled that promise by making God's salvation possible for people of all nations. Abraham is also called the father of all believers (Rom. 4:11-12; see Gal. 3:29).

Aramaic—one of the common languages used in Palestine during the time of Jesus' public ministry.

baptism—In the ministry of John the Baptist, this was an outward sign indicating repentance on the part of the sinner who wanted to be forgiven (Mark 1:4; Acts 19:1-5). Baptism in Christ is a sign of the inward washing away of sin and the dying of the sinful nature to rebirth and renewal (Acts 22:16; Rom. 6:1-4; Titus 3:4). This sacrament is usually performed by sprinkling with or by immersion in water.

blasphemy—scoffing at or misusing the name of God. The Jewish leaders accused Jesus of blasphemy because he claimed to be God, and they refused to believe him.

the Christ—see **Messiah**.

David—a shepherd boy from Bethlehem who became one of the greatest kings of ancient Israel. He wrote many psalms and established the worship of God in Jerusalem. (See 1 Sam. 16:1-1 Kings 2:12.) According to God's promise in 2 Samuel 7, the Messiah would be a descendant of David.

eternal life—life that lasts forever with God. It begins when one receives Jesus by faith as Savior, and it reaches fulfillment in the new heaven and earth when the believer's soul is reunited with his or her resurrected body to live in God's presence forever (1 Cor. 15:20-54).

the Father—the first person of the Trinity. The other two persons are God the Son (Jesus Christ) and God the Holy Spirit. They are three persons in one being.

Feast of Dedication—a winter celebration commemorating the rededication of the Jewish temple in Jerusalem after a defeat of Greek oppressors in 164 B.C. This feast is also known as Hanukkah or the Festival of Lights.

Feast of Tabernacles—a fall harvest festival commemorating God's covenant with Israel during their stay in the wilderness after being freed from slavery in Egypt. This was one of three annual feasts that all Jewish males were required to attend; the other two were the Feast of Passover and the Feast of Weeks (Pentecost).

Galilee—the northernmost province of ancient Palestine. It was separated from Judea by Samaria, and the Aramaic dialect of this region was noticeably different from the Aramaic spoken in Judea. It was also an area where many Gentiles lived. Most Jews in the south thought Galilee was on the fringe of Judaism, both culturally and spiritually. Jesus grew up in the village of Nazareth in Galilee, and a great deal of his public ministry took place in this region.

glory—splendor, majesty, power, worth, excellence of quality and character. Jesus revealed God's glory and his unity with God through his teaching and miracles (John 2:11) and through his death and resurrection.

gospel—This word literally means "good news" and refers to the message of God's salvation from sin and the promise of eternal life through Jesus Christ. This word can also refer to one of the first four books of the New Testament (Matthew, Mark, Luke, and John) that tell the good news story about Jesus.

grace—God's undeserved favor and forgiving love. Jesus is the full expression of God's grace "in the flesh" for the salvation of all who believe in him as Lord and Savior.

Greeks—another name for Gentiles who lived in Israel and who mainly spoke Greek as a result of Greek influence over the region since the time of Alexander the Great (331 B.C.).

Holy Spirit—the third person of the Trinity. The other two persons are God the Father and God the Son (Jesus Christ). They are three persons in one being.

Isaiah—one of the major prophets of Israel. Isaiah prophesied from 740-681 B.C. and delivered a number of clear prophecies about the Messiah of Israel.

Jacob—grandson of Abraham and father of the twelve tribes of Israel. God renamed him Israel, which means "he struggles with God" (see Gen. 32:28). Jacob bought some land near Sychar and dug a well there (John 4:5-6). The land was given to the descendants of Jacob's son Joseph, and in Jesus' day this well was in Samaritan territory.

Jerusalem—the capital of Judea and the religious center for all Jews. The temple was located there.

Jewish ruling council—see **Sanhedrin.**

Jews—descendants of the Israelite tribes of (mainly) Judah and Benjamin who returned from exile in Babylon to rebuild Jerusalem and the temple of the Lord after 538 B.C. The gospel writer John uses this term frequently, sometimes to refer to the Jewish people but most often to refer to the Jewish religious leaders in Jerusalem.

John the Baptist—the last prophet who called people to repentance to help them prepare for the coming of the Messiah. John baptized people in the Jordan River as a symbol of their repentance and preparation. John was also Jesus' cousin. (See Luke 1:5-66; 3:1-6, 15-20.)

John the disciple—a close friend and disciple of Jesus who wrote the gospel of John. He also wrote three letters and the book of Revelation in the New Testament.

Lamb of God—John the Baptist used this phrase to describe Jesus at the time of his baptism as he began his public ministry (John 1:29, 35). This title implied that Jesus as Messiah would be a sacrificial substitute for sins (based on traditional sacrifices for Passover and atonement for sin—Ex. 12; Lev. 16; see also Heb. 10:1-18).

the Law (and the Prophets)—In Jesus' day people often used this term to refer to the body of Old Testament writings that made up the Jewish Scriptures (see Matt. 5:17; 22:40).

manna—a food that God provided for the Israelites during their travels in the desert after their release from slavery in Egypt. The manna appeared on the ground each morning, except on the Sabbath, and could be used for baking bread. Many of the Jews believed the Messiah would renew the sending of this "bread from heaven" (see John 6:32-35).

Messiah—the promised deliverer of God's people. Both the Hebrew word *Messiah* and the Greek word *Christ* mean "Anointed One." Through the prophets God promised to send the Messiah to deliver God's people from evil oppressors and to rule them in righteousness forever. The people misunderstood these promises, however, and looked for a Messiah who would be a political ruler and gather an army to rout all their physical enemies. But as Jesus revealed through his work and teaching, the Messiah came to save God's people from the oppression of sin and death and to give them new life forever with God. He rules today in heaven at the right hand of the Father, and when he comes again at the end of time he will fully establish God's everlasting kingdom of righteousness on earth. (See Matt. 26:63-64; John 16:5-16; 1 Cor. 15; Rev. 21:1-5; 22:1-5.)

money changers—officials who exchanged Roman currency into the Jewish currency acceptable to temple authorities for the payment of offerings and temple taxes.

Moses—the leader of the Israelites when God delivered them from slavery in Egypt and as they lived in the wilderness before entering the promised land (Palestine). Moses received the law from God and taught it to the Israelites.

Passover—This feast took place each spring to celebrate the Israelites' exodus from slavery in Egypt. The name commemorates God's protection of Israelite households during a final plague sent to convince the Egyptian king (pharaoh) to let the Israelites go. God promised that upon seeing the blood of a sacrificed lamb on the doorframes of a house, God would *pass over* that house and not allow the plague of death to take the life of the firstborn in that house (see Ex. 12).

Pharisees—an elite group that emphasized precise obedience to scriptural and traditional law. A number of Pharisees were part of the Sanhedrin (the Jewish ruling council).

priests—officials who served in the temple and belonged to the tribe of Levi; also often called Levites.

Pool of Siloam—a pool at the southern end of Jerusalem.

the Prophet—In Deuteronomy 18:15-19 Moses describes this person whom God promised to raise up to teach the people in the name of the Lord. While other great prophets such as Elijah, Isaiah, Jeremiah, and John the Baptist served God faithfully and filled this description in some ways, Jesus is the ultimate fulfillment of this promise.

rabbi—a Jewish religious scholar and teacher. Well-known rabbis often had disciples.

Sabbath—the seventh day of the week (Saturday), set aside as a day of rest and restoration according to the law of Moses. Jewish religious leaders developed a stringent code of rules for keeping the Sabbath, and Jesus often criticized them for being too legalistic in this regard (see Mark 2:23-3:6; Luke 13:10-17; John 5:16-17; 7:21-24).

Samaritans—residents of Samaria who descended from the ten northern tribes of Israel. The Samaritans had intermarried with other peoples in the region and claimed that God was to be worshiped at Mount Gerizim, not in Jerusalem. They despised the Jews (who descended from the two southern tribes of Judah and Benjamin), and the Jews despised them.

Sanhedrin—the ruling council of the Jews, made up of seventy-one officials including Pharisees, Sadducees, leading elders, legal experts, and priests. Nicodemus was a member of this group (John 3:1), and so was Joseph of Arimathea (Mark 15:43; John 19:38-42).

Satan—this name means "accuser" (see Zech. 3:1) and refers to the fallen angel who tempted humanity to sin and wants to destroy God's kingdom. The Bible refers to this being as "the evil one" (Matt. 6:13); "a roaring lion looking for someone to devour" (1 Pet. 5:8); "the great dragon . . . that ancient serpent called the devil, Satan, who leads the whole world astray" (Rev. 12:9); "the prince of this world" who "now stands condemned" (John 16:11); and more. When Jesus conquered sin and death for our sake, he dealt Satan a fatal blow (see Gen. 3:14-15) and destroyed Satan's power to accuse us of our sins before God (Col. 2:13-15). At the end of time, Jesus will completely defeat Satan (Rev. 20:7-10). Though Satan is still powerful and dangerous today, he cannot snatch us from God's hand (John 10:27-30).

Sea of Galilee—a large freshwater lake in Galilee that was also known as the Sea of Tiberias (after a town on its western coast, named for a Roman caesar—see John 6:1, 23; 21:1).

Son of God—Jesus used this term to describe his relationship as God the Son with God the Father. The Jewish leaders clearly understood this term to mean having equality with God.

Son of Man—Jesus used this term to describe his humanity as well as to refer to a title associated with the Messiah as described by the prophet Daniel (see Dan. 7:13-14; Matt. 24:30; 25:31; 26:64).

Spirit—see **Holy Spirit**.

synagogue—the local gathering place for weekly services in Jewish communities. There were many synagogues throughout Palestine, but the only temple was in Jerusalem.

temple—the religious center of Judaism in the Old Testament and in Jesus' day. Located in Jerusalem, it was the place of worship and sacrifice, the site of major Jewish festivals, and the gathering place of religious thinkers, teachers, and leaders.

the Twelve—another name for Jesus' twelve disciples.

the Word—In the original Greek language of John's text, the word *logos* (translated as "Word") could have several meanings. Greek philosophers often used this word to refer to the unifying force of the universe. Given the context of statements like "In him all things were made" and "In him was life" (John 1:3-4), we can see that John was using *logos* to speak of Jesus as the divine Word who holds all things together (see also Col. 1:15-20).

Lesson 1

John 11

From Death to Life—for God's Glory

Additional Related Scriptures

Psalm 66:18

Matthew 26:3-5

Luke 7:11-17; 8:51-56; 10:38-39;
    11:9-13

John 1:1-2, 5, 10-12, 16-18, 29; 3:16,
    19-21; 4:34; 5:16, 18, 21-29; 6:38,
    40-42, 54, 66; 7:1, 27, 30-32, 45, 52;
    8:12, 23-27, 47-59; 9:4-5, 31, 39;
    10:22-33, 39, 40-42; 20:24-28

Introductory Notes

Many people assume that if only they could witness a miracle from
God, they would believe in God. But as this lesson shows, many skeptics
refused to believe in Jesus as God even though he brought a dead man back
to life.

John 11 describes one of the most amazing miracles of Jesus: he raised
his friend Lazarus from the grave although he had been dead for four days.
In this episode we also see Jesus "deeply moved . . . and troubled" in spirit,
so affected by the death of his friend that he wept openly (John 11:33, 35).

The Son of God cares so deeply for us that he came to conquer death for
our sake and offer us full life with God forever. As you study this lesson
together, ask God for the wisdom to share with others how this offer from
God still stands.

1.   *John 11:1-6*

Note: You may want to read or review together the full narrative of the
death and resurrection of Lazarus (John 11:1-44) before discussing the
following questions. Some details mentioned later in the story shed light on
events described at the beginning. In addition, a review of John 10:40-42 can
help recall the setting in which part of the story takes place.

a.   What do we learn about Mary, Martha, and Lazarus? Describe their
relationship to Jesus.

13

b. What message did the sisters send to Jesus, and what was his response?

2. *John 11:7-16*

   a. Why didn't the disciples want Jesus to go back to Judea?

   b. How did Jesus answer them?

   c. How did Thomas react?

3. *John 11:17-27*

   a. Describe the scene as Jesus arrived in Bethany.

b. What did Martha say to Jesus, and what did she mean?

c. Did she understand Jesus' response about Lazarus rising again?

5. *John 11:28-37*
   a. What did Mary do when Martha said Jesus was asking for her?

   b. How did Jesus react to the situation?

   c. How did the mourners react to the fact that Jesus wept?

6. *John 11:38-44*

   What happened at the tomb?

7. *John 11:45-57*

   a. What were the people's reactions to the raising of Lazarus?

   b. Did Caiaphas know what he was saying?

   c. What did the Jewish leaders plan to do, and how did Jesus respond?

Questions for Reflection

   What does the story of Lazarus teach us about death?

What does it teach about Jesus and who he is?

Think about sharing this story with someone you know who doesn't know Jesus. What would you say?

Lesson 2
John 12:1-19

Worship, Honor, and Unbelief

Additional Related Scriptures

Deuteronomy 15:11
Psalm 118:25-27
Zechariah 9:9-10
Matthew 21:1-11; 25:37-40
Mark 11:1-11

Luke 19:29-44; 24:27
John 11:47-48
Acts 1:6-9; 2:1-39
Philippians 2:9-11

Introductory Notes

People respond to the person of Jesus in many ways, and this lesson covers a range of those responses. The story about Mary anointing Jesus with oil stands out in Scripture as an extravagant act of devotion. She shows herself to be, as some would say, "sold out for Christ."

In this lesson we also see people who follow Jesus only when it suits their purpose. The crowds, for example, honor him gladly, thinking he will bring them physical or political relief. But as we will see in later lessons, these same crowds reject Jesus a few days later and call for his execution.

Lurking in the shadows are others who have never understood Jesus. Their own sinful choices make it impossible for them to understand the real message and mission of Jesus (John 3:16-21). As a result, they reject him and try to stop others from following him.

1. *John 12:1-6*

   a. Why is Jesus in Bethany, and what is he celebrating?

   b. What does Mary do?

c. Describe Judas's behavior in response to that of Mary.

2. *John 12:7-11*

   a. How does Jesus interpret Mary's actions?

   b. Given the way Jesus has treated people in need, what does he mean in his remarks about the poor?

   c. What do the chief priests plan to do? Why?

3. *John 12:12-16*

   a. How does the crowd in Jerusalem greet Jesus and why?

   b. What's the significance of the way Jesus rides into Jerusalem?

c. When did Jesus' disciples understand the meaning of all this? Why?

4. *John 12:17-19*

  a. How did the raising of Lazarus influence the crowd?

  b. Why were the religious leaders so frustrated?

Questions for Reflection

  In what ways can you show your devotion to Christ?

  If you had been in the crowd when Jesus rode into Jerusalem, how do you think you would have responded?

Lesson 3
John 12:20-50

Drawn to True Life

Additional Related Scriptures

Psalm 89:36; 110:1-4
Isaiah 6:3, 8-13; 9:6-7; 49:5-7; 52:13-
53:12
Daniel 7:13-14

Mathew 10:39
Luke 23:20-23
John 5:19-30; 6:35-40; 8:12-47; 9:4-5;
10:25-30; 11:9-10

Introductory Notes

In the Scripture passage for this lesson, Jesus talks about people believing in him and being drawn to him. We meet Greek believers who want to know more about Jesus, and we learn that "many even among the [Jewish] leaders" believe in Jesus but are afraid to stand up for him (12:42). These are people whom the Father is gradually drawing to himself (John 6:44), and Jesus explains that this process calls for him to be "lifted up from the earth" (12:32), meaning he will die on a cross for the sake of all who will believe in him as Savior (see 3:14-16).

Give thanks together that although we are weak-willed and often fearful, Jesus came to stand up for us. He came to take our place by suffering and dying for our sin. Because of Jesus' faithfulness, we are able to change radically to serve God instead of ourselves, and we are able to enjoy the gift of eternal life—to the Father's glory.

1. *John 12:20-26*

   a. Who wished to see Jesus, and why didn't they approach him directly?

   greeks
   THEY WERE JEWISH CONVENTS &
   went to Phillip who went to Andrew

   b. How did Jesus respond?

21

    c.   What does it mean to "hate" our life and "keep" it for eternal life?

2. *John 12:27-33*
    a.   Why was Jesus troubled, and what was his prayer?

    b.   How did God respond?

    c.   What did Jesus tell the crowd?

3. *John 12:34-36*
    How did the crowd respond to Jesus' announcement?

4. *John 12:37-43*

    a.   What reason does John give to explain why many of the people in Jesus' day refused to believe in him?

    b.   Why did the leaders who believed in Jesus fear the Pharisees?

5. *John 12:44-50*

    a.   What happens when a person believes in Jesus?

    b.   What does Jesus say about judgment?

    c.   Who directs Jesus' teaching?

Question for Reflection

Now that you've studied the second half of John 12, reflect again on the people's reactions to Jesus and what it might have been like to have been there. How do you think you would have responded to Jesus?

Lesson 4
John 13

An Example of Love

Additional Related Scriptures

Leviticus 19:18
Deuteronomy 18:21-22
Psalm 41:9; 51:2, 7
Isaiah 1:16-20
Matthew 26:14-35
Mark 12:30-31; 14:12-31
Luke 9:44-45; 18:31-34; 22:7-34,
    69-70

John 7:33-36; 11:33; 12:6, 16, 23,
    27-28, 41; 14:16, 26; 16:7-14; 15:16,
    26-27; 17:1, 6-19, 20-23; 19:26; 20:2
Acts 1:6-9; 2:31-36
Romans 5:8, 10
Philippians 2:6-15
1 Peter 5:8
Revelation 12:7-12

Introductory Notes

We all have had jobs that we think are beneath us. But Jesus considered no job too low for serving as an example of God's love. In John 13 we find the amazing episode in which Jesus took a basin of water and a towel and washed his disciples' feet. These moments were among his last hours with his disciples, and he wanted to provide an indelible picture of true servanthood.

In this passage Jesus also predicts his painful betrayal by Judas as well as Peter's denial of him. Jesus felt the pang of rejection even within his circle of closest followers, all of whom eventually left him to complete the hardest part of his mission alone. Whenever we go through the pain of rejection or betrayal, we can be assured that Jesus knows our pain—and that he cares.

As John 13:1 explains by way of introduction, this section covers Jesus' final evening with his friends (John 13-17) as well as his death and resurrection:

> It was just before the Passover Feast. Jesus knew that the time had come for him to leave this world and go to the Father. Having loved his own who were in the world, he now showed them the full extent of his love.

1. *John 13:1-3*

Describe the setting portrayed in these opening verses of John 13.

2. *John 13:4-17*

   a. What did Jesus do here for his disciples, and why?

   b. Why did Peter resist at first?

   c. What changed Peter's mind? Why did he need to allow Jesus to wash his feet?

   d. Who was clean and who was not? Why?

   e. What else did Jesus say to explain his washing of everyone's feet?

3. *John 13:18-30*

   a. What's the significance of the Scripture that Jesus quoted here?

   b. What explanation did Jesus give about what would soon happen?

   c. How did Jesus as well as his disciples react when he said this?

4. *John 13:31-38*

   a. What did Jesus mean when he spoke about God and the Son of Man being glorified?

   b. What command did Jesus give his disciples, and how was it new?

c. How did Peter view his loyalty to Jesus, and what did Jesus say about it?

Question for Reflection

What can we learn from the words and actions of Jesus in the episode covered in this lesson? From the words and actions of the disciples?

Lesson 5
John 14

"I Am the Way and the Truth and the Life"

Additional Related Scriptures

Exodus 3:14-15; 12:1-42; 20:7;
  33:17-23
Leviticus 24:16
Matthew 10:3
Mark 3:18
Luke 6:16

John 1:29, 32-34; 3:16; 4:21-24;
  5:17-40; 6:35-58; 7:37-38; 8:12, 34;
  9:5; 10:7-18, 24-30, 37-38;
  11:25-26; 12:26, 44-50; 13:12-19,
  21, 28, 34; 15:1, 5, 12-17; 16:7-15
Acts 1:13; 2:1-4:22
Galatians 5:13-16, 22-25
Philippians 2:6-11

Introductory Notes

In this lesson we find words of tremendous comfort in the midst of important teachings. Jesus spoke these words first to his disciples, but these sayings have provided comfort to all generations of Jesus' followers.

It was the night before he was crucified, and Jesus said to his followers, "Let not your hearts be troubled. Trust in God; trust also in me" (John 14:1). Then he proceeded to teach about his going to prepare a place for them in heaven, saying, "I am the way and the truth and the life. No one comes to the Father except through me" (14:6). Jesus had made several other "I am" statements before, and we'll be exploring those in some detail in this lesson. As we've mentioned in earlier lessons, Jesus' use of this construction made clear to his listeners that he was claiming to be God. And in the statement he makes here he sets himself apart from all other religious leaders. This is the teaching from which the Christian church learns that belief in Jesus is the only way to eternal life with God.

In the Scripture for this lesson Jesus also introduces the Holy Spirit as "the Counselor" who will come to be with his followers after Jesus goes away (14:16, 26). It's important to know that the word for "Counselor" (*parakleton*) in this passage can be translated more literally as "Comforter." With these words of comfort Jesus' disciples also receive a glimpse of the close relationship between the persons of the Trinity—Father, Son, and Holy Spirit—and how they work together to provide us the assurance of God's love and peace and eternal life.

1. *John 14:1-4*

    a. Why did Jesus tell his disciples not to be troubled?

    b. What does Jesus promise to provide for his disciples?

2. *John 14:5-11*

    a. What does Thomas claim, and how does Jesus respond?

    b. Why would Jesus make such an exclusive claim (v. 6)?

    c. What is the meaning of Philip's request in verse 8?

3. *John 14:12-14*

    a. What does Jesus tell his disciples they will be able to do?

    b. What great promise does Jesus give in verse 13?

4. *John 14:15-27*

    a. What will result if the disciples love Jesus?

    b. How will this connect with the work of the Holy Spirit?

    c. How does "Judas (not Iscariot)" respond, and what does Jesus say to him?

    d.   What kind of peace is Jesus promising in verse 27?

5.   *John 14:28-31*

    a.   Why would the disciples be glad that Jesus is going away?

    b.   What must the world learn about Jesus? Why?

Questions for Reflection

How can we share with others the essential truth that Jesus is only way to salvation?

What can we do to share the peace of Christ with others?

Lesson 6
John 15

The True Vine

Additional Related Scriptures

Psalm 35:19; 69:4; 109:3
Isaiah 5:1-7
Jeremiah 12:2, 10
Ezekiel 19:10-14
Matthew 21:33-41
John 1:1, 14; 3:19-20; 6:44; 11:48;
    12:32, 37-40; 13:16, 34-35;
    14:6, 12-16, 21-26

Acts 1:8; 7:54-8:3; 9:1-2
Romans 12
1 Corinthians 3:11-15; 12:1-31
Ephesians 2:10; 4:7-16
Galatians 5:22-25
1 John 4:19

Introductory Notes

Jesus knew that his time with his disciples was short. Within a few hours he would be arrested and sentenced to be crucified, so he wanted to give his followers some important words of instruction, warning, and comfort. Many of these words repeat teachings he gave earlier, but in this passage Jesus offers great comfort by describing himself as "the true vine" (John 15:1) to which all believers can remain connected through the life and guidance of the Holy Spirit. Jesus knew the challenges his followers would face when he was arrested and crucified, and he knew how they would struggle and persevere in God's strength in the years ahead.

1. *John 15:1-8*

a. Explain the word picture Jesus uses in these verses.

b. What does it mean to remain in Jesus?

STAY in me, + I will STAY w you

no Branch can bear fruit by itself
Remain
Must remain in the true Vine

33

c. What is the condition for the promise in verse 7, and what is
    the result?

*Remain in me + my words
remain in you*

2. *John 15:9-17*
    a. How has Jesus loved us?

*As my Father has loved me so
I will & him you*

    b. Why should we love each other?

*So we will have the love of our
father*

    c. What has Jesus chosen us to do?

Love each other

3. *John 15:18-25*
    a. What should we remember when the world rejects us?

It. hated them first so same as us

16:7

b. Why is the persecution of Jesus and his disciples inexcusable?

JESUS MUST show that the world had
to see his sacrifices - Healing people
+ Recovering the dead -
Doing these things only God can do
& He is

c. What does Jesus mean when he says, "He who hates me hates my Father as well" (v. 23)?

HumAn Too

NON BELIEVERS

d. How does the world's hatred of Jesus fulfill the law?

SAW WHAT HE DID Y

4. John 15:26-27

a. What do we learn about the Counselor in this passage?

b. Why must the disciples testify?

Questions for Reflection

What kinds of things need to be present in your life to help you remain in Christ?

With whom can you share the message and love of Christ today?

Lesson 7
John 16

The Counselor

Additional Related Scriptures

Matthew 16:15-19
Luke 24:27, 44-49
John 6:39-40, 69-70; 13:36; 14:6, 27;
    15:20, 26; 20:10-21:14
Acts 1:1-3; 2:1-4:37; 7:54-8:3; 8:26-40;
    9:1-2; 10:1-11:18; 13:1-3; 15:22-32

Romans 3:22-25
Colossians 2:13-15
2 Timothy 3:16-17
1 John 3:8
Revelation 19:11-22:5

Introductory Notes

Jesus continues to prepare his followers for the difficulties they will soon face when he is arrested and crucified. He compares their time of grief to a woman in childbirth, who labors in great difficulty for a time and then experiences great joy when her child is born. Jesus also again promises to send the Counselor, the Holy Spirit, who will come to be with them and live in them. The Spirit will supply them with peace so that the disciples may "take heart" when they face tough times; through the Spirit, Jesus' followers can be assured that he has "overcome the world" (John 16:33).

1. *John 16:1-4*

    What will soon happen to the disciples, and why does Jesus tell them this?

2. *John 16:5-11*

    a. Why will Jesus' leaving be good for his followers?

b. In what ways will the Counselor influence the world?

3. *John 16:12-16*

What will the Spirit of truth do for Jesus' followers?

4. *John 16:17-24*

a. What are the disciples wondering about here?

b. How does Jesus respond to their confusion?

5. *John 16:25-33*

a. Why has Jesus been speaking figuratively to his disciples?

b. What relationship do the disciples have with the Father?

c. How do the disciples respond to Jesus' explanation?

d. What does Jesus say next, and what does this mean?

e. What assurance does Jesus give in these parting words to his disciples?

Questions for Reflection

In what ways has Jesus prepared his followers for the challenges they will be facing?

How do his words prepare us as well?

Lesson 8
John 17

Final Prayers

Additional Related Scriptures

Psalm 20:1; 54:1
Proverbs 18:10
Matthew 6:9-13; 10:19-20
John 1:1-4, 10-14; 13:18-30;
    15:8-16:4, 32-33

Acts 2:42-27; 4:32-35
Ephesians 2:6
Philippians 2:5-11

Introductory Notes

Perhaps you have known the comfort of being prayed for at one time or another. Perhaps a family member or friend has spoken to God on your behalf. You may even be aware that you've been prayed for countless times. In this lesson we have the privilege of listening to Jesus pray that God will work through him, through his disciples, and through all believers who will come after them. That includes all believers throughout the centuries—even us who are believers today. What's more, the Bible also teaches that Jesus and the Holy Spirit keep praying for us throughout our lives. Amazing! (See Rom. 8:26-27, 34; Heb. 7:25; 1 John 2:1.)

1. *John 17:1-5*

   a. What does Jesus ask for in these verses?

   b. How does Jesus describe eternal life in this passage?

c. What does Jesus acknowledge about himself in verses 4-5?

2. *John 17:6-12*
   a. What has Jesus revealed, and how has he done this?

   b. Why is Jesus praying for his disciples but not for the world?

   c. What does Jesus want for the disciples that he has experienced with his Father?

   d. What does Jesus' prayer tell us about being kept safe and being lost?

3. *John 17:13-19*

    What do the disciples need to be protected from, and how will they be protected?

4. *John 17:20-23*

    a. Who does Jesus now include in his prayer, and what does he pray for them?

    b. What is the purpose of the oneness of all who believe?

5. *John 17:24-26*

    a. What additional prayer requests does Jesus make on our behalf?

    b. What will Jesus continue to reveal to those who believe in him?

Questions for Reflection

What difference does it make in your life to know Jesus has prayed these prayers for you?

What can you do in response to Jesus' prayers and show the unifying love of God in this world?

Lesson 9
John 18

Jesus' Arrest

Additional Related Scriptures

Matthew 26:36-27:26   John 7:6, 30; 8:20; 10:39; 12:23, 27;
Mark 14:32-15:15   13:1; 17:1
Luke 22:39-23:19

Introductory Notes

John 18 begins with Jesus and his disciples going to an olive grove, where Judas soon leads the Jewish authorities to arrest him. John leaves it to the other gospel writers to mention Jesus' anguish as he struggles there with God to let the suffering of the cross pass from him (Luke 22:39-46). During this time Jesus asks his Father if there might be another way to save the world, but this is one prayer of the Son to which the Father answers no.

The story of Jesus' passion shows that in his obedience he is willing to submit humbly to betrayal, torture, and even death. The religious leaders and Roman authorities may think they are in charge, but it is Jesus and the Father who are in control. As he said when teaching about laying down his life for his sheep, "The reason my Father loves me is that I lay down my life—only to take it up again. No one takes it from me, but I lay it down of my own accord. I have authority to lay it down and authority to take it up again" (John 10:17-18).

1. *John 18:1-11*

   a. How does Jesus show he is in charge of the situation surrounding his arrest?

   b. What is Jesus' concern for his disciples, and how does he show it?

18:11

c. Why does Jesus say, "Shall I not drink the cup the Father has given me?"

Suffering, ISOLATION + DEATH. that Jesus would have to endure in order to atone for the sins of the world

2. *John 18:12-27*

a. Where and how is Jesus taken?

Bound him + took him to ANNAS, (ALSO Father in law of Caiaphas   former high PRIEST

b. Who follows Jesus and why?

18: 15, 16

Simon peter + probably JOHN: AUTHOR OF THIS gospel They knew the High priest Caia Caiaphas

c. What happens to Peter in the high priest's courtyard?

Ask whether he was a disciple + ANSWER: 'I am not'

d. What happens during Jesus' hearing with the high priest?

e. How does Peter respond when he is questioned again?

WAS ASKED "You are not one of the
desciples "ARE you"? DENIED "I AM NOT
High PRIEST SERVANT challed him."
Did I NOT see you with him in the olive grove
+ peter said again denied it

3. John 18:28-32

a. Where is Jesus taken next, and why don't the Jewish leaders follow along? AFTER CAIAPHAS - led him to the palace to the Roman Governor. PILATE

b. Discuss the exchange between Pilate and the Jewish leaders. PILATE came out to address the Jewish leaders 18:28 Jewish law, enter the house of gentile would cause a Jewls person to be eremoniously unclean defiled

4. John 18:33-40

a. Describe the conversation between Pilate and Jesus.

b. What tactics does Pilate use in his attempt to save Jesus from death?

Questions for Reflection

If you had been one of Jesus' disciples, how do you think you would have reacted to his arrest and trial? In what ways can you identify with Peter?

In what circumstances can you be bold in identifying with Jesus? In what circumstances are you fearful?

Use these questions both for review and for reflection on circumstances that might make it easy or difficult to stand up for Jesus. Think about whether it's easier to defend Jesus on the spur of the moment or after you've had time to think up a response.

Lesson 10
John 19

"It Is Finished"

Additional Related Scriptures

Exodus 12:46
Leviticus 24:16
Numbers 9:12
Deuteronomy 21:22-23
Psalm 22; 34:20; 69:21
Isaiah 53
Zechariah 12:10

Matthew 26:52-54; 27:27-61
Mark 15:9-10, 15-47
Luke 23:18-56
John 1:29; 3:1-21; 7:45-52; 10:17-18;
    11:45-53
Galatians 3:13
Hebrews 12:2

Introductory Notes

John 19 describes the sentencing, death, and burial of Jesus, "the Lamb of God, who takes away the sin of the world" (John 1:29). Jesus' death is probably the most studied death in the history of the world, because Christians believe that his death pays the debt of their sin, freeing them to begin new life with God forever. As Romans 6:23 says, "The wages of sin is death, but the gift of God is eternal life in Christ Jesus our Lord." Because Christ laid down his perfect life for our sake, God considers us righteous for his sake. If we believe this good news that the finished work of Christ can save us from eternal death (the penalty of sin), we gain "the right to become children of God" (John 1:12) and have eternal life. As you study this chapter of John, remind yourself that even though Jesus' death was sufficient to save the whole world (John 3:16), his death was also for you personally.

1. *John 19:1-11*

    a.   Why do you think Pilate has Jesus flogged?

    b.   What's the significance of the soldiers' treatment of Jesus?

c. Why is Jesus condemned if Pilate has found no basis for a charge against him?

d. How does Jesus respond to Pilate's comment about his power as a Roman governor?

2. *John 19:12-16*
What do the Jewish leaders remind Pilate of in verse 12?

3. *John 19:17-22*
   a. Describe the scene of Jesus' crucifixion.

   b. What was the significance of Christ's death on a cross?

4. *John 19:23-27*

    a.   What prophecy is fulfilled when the soldiers take Jesus' clothes?

    b.   What does Jesus do when he sees his mother standing next to John?

5. *John 19:28-37*

    a.   How do these verses describe the final words of Jesus and the end of his mission?

    b.   Discuss what occurred next, along with the meaning of the prophecies in verses 36-37.

6. *John 19:38-42*

    What's the significance of Jesus' burial place and the role of Joseph and Nicodemus in burying Jesus' body?

Question for Reflection

As an exercise that can help you tell this story to someone who hasn't heard it before, imagine yourself to be one of the individuals present at Jesus' crucifixion and describe what you would have seen and experienced and how you might have felt.

Lesson 11
John 20

Risen from the Dead!

Additional Related Scriptures

Matthew 28
Mark 16
Luke 23:54; 24:1-49
John 11:16, 25-26; 19:42
Acts 1-2

Romans 3:21-5:5; 10:17
1 Corinthians 15:42-49
2 Corinthians 5:17-21
Philippians 3:20-21
Hebrews 11:1, 7-28

Introductory Notes

When he spoke with Mary of Bethany as she grieved the death of her brother, Jesus said, "I am the resurrection and the life. He who believes in me will live, even though he dies; and whoever lives and believes in me will never die" (John 11:25-26). The account of Jesus' own resurrection in John 20 shows that this was no empty promise. Because Jesus came back to life, we have the living hope that we too, even if we die, will live again someday—and that our life in him begins even now (John 20:31; 2 Cor. 5:17; Phil. 3:20; 1 Pet. 1:3-9).

1. *John 20:1-9*

Note: Mary Magdalene has often become a figure of interest in religious history, and renewed intrigue about her life and character has surfaced again recently. Most of the hype, however, is fictional. What we know from the Bible is that Mary Magdalene was a woman whom Jesus healed of demon possession and who became one of his followers (Mark 16:9; Luke 8:1-3). She even helped to support Jesus' ministry out of her own financial resources (Luke 8:2-3). Some people have thought she was the woman in John 8 who was caught in adultery, and some have speculated that she was the "woman who had lived a sinful life" and interrupted a party to wash Jesus' feet as portrayed in Luke 7:36-50. Though some movies have portrayed her that way, Scripture does not support that perspective. Further, nothing in Scripture indicates a romantic connection between Mary Magdalene and Jesus, as some dramatizations and novels have suggested.

Probably the most significant (though often overlooked) fact about Mary Magdalene is that, according to the Bible, she was the first person to whom Jesus appeared after his resurrection (Mark 16:9; John 20:1, 10-16) and with whom he entrusted the good news that he had risen (20:17-18). Another significant fact is that she and other women are mentioned consistently and prominently as witnesses to the resurrection. These facts actually help to testify to the truth of Jesus' resurrection. Considering that women were not perceived as reliable witnesses in Jesus' day (for example, they could not testify in a court of law), scholars have noted that if anyone in those days had wanted to fabricate the story of Jesus' resurrection, they would not have claimed women as the first witnesses.

    a.   When did Mary go to the tomb, and what did she discover there?

    b.   How did Peter and John respond when Mary spoke to them?

2.   *John 20:10-18*
    a.   What occurred when Mary remained at the tomb?

    b.   What happened when Mary turned around?

3. *John 20:19-23*

    a. Describe what happened when Jesus appeared to the disciples.

    b. What additional words of encouragement did Jesus give the disciples?

4. *John 20:24-29*

    a. Give a character sketch of Thomas.

    b. Can you identify in any way with how Thomas felt? Why or why not?

    c. How did Thomas respond to Jesus?

d. What did Jesus say about others who will believe?

5. *John 20:30-31*

    a. What information does John add in these verses?

    b. Why has John written this book?

Question for Reflection

What's your response to this book John has written? How would you describe it to others?

Lesson 12
John 21

"Follow Me!"

Additional Related Scriptures

Matthew 26:33-34; 28:10
Mark 16:7
Luke 5:1-11

John 6:1-15; 10:11, 14-16; 12:27-28;
  13:37-38; 15:8, 18-21; 16:7-16;
  17:13-26; 18:17, 25-27
Galatians 2:11-13
1 Peter 1:1-9; 5:1-4

Introductory Notes

On the Sea of Tiberias (Sea of Galilee) after a long night of fishing without a catch, a group of Jesus' disciples are returning to shore in the early morning. There's a man on shore whom they fail to recognize at first. The man is Jesus, and he still has some things to teach his disciples. In this closing chapter of John's gospel account, Jesus again teaches as clearly with his actions as with his words. And he provides an amazing model for relational ministry, servant leadership, and forgiveness.

1. *John 21:1-6*

   a. Who's been out fishing, and what has gone wrong?

   b. Who is standing on shore, and what does he tell them?

2. *John 21:7-14*

    a.   Who recognizes the Lord, and what does Peter do in response?

    b.   What's significant about the abundant catch of fish?

    c.   When the disciples reach shore, what do they see?

3. *John 21:15-17*

    a.   What does Jesus ask Peter after they have finished eating?

    b.   In response to Peter's answers, what does Jesus tell Peter to do?

4. *John 21:18-19*

    a.   What prediction does Jesus make about Peter?

    b.   What's the significance of Jesus' saying, "Follow me!"

5. *John 21:20-23*

What distracts Peter next, and how does Jesus respond?

6. *John 21:24-25*

What does John want to communicate as he closes this book?

Questions for Reflection

How has your life been affected by studying the eyewitness account of Jesus as written by John?

In what ways has this study helped to prepare you to spread the good news to others?

Are you called to tend the flock and feed the sheep of the good shepherd? Explain.

An Invitation

Listen now to what God is saying to you.

You may be aware of things in your life that keep you from coming near to God. You may have thought of God as someone who is unsympathetic, angry, and punishing. You may feel as if you don't know how to pray or how to come near to God.

"But because of his great love for us, God, who is rich in mercy, made us alive with Christ even when we were dead in transgressions—it is by grace you have been saved" (Eph. 2:4-5). Jesus, God's Son, died on the cross to save us from our sins. It doesn't matter where you come from, what you've done in the past, or what your heritage is. God has been watching over you and caring for you, drawing you closer. "You also were included in Christ when you heard the word of truth, the gospel of your salvation" (Eph. 1:13).

Do you want to receive Jesus as your Savior and Lord? It's as simple as A-B-C:

- **A**dmit that you have sinned and that you need God's forgiveness.
- **B**elieve that God loves you and that Jesus has already paid the price for your sins.
- **C**ommit your life to God in prayer, asking the Lord to forgive your sins, nurture you as his child, and fill you with the Holy Spirit.

Prayer of Commitment

Here is a prayer of commitment recognizing Jesus Christ as Savior. If you long to be in a loving relationship with Jesus, pray this prayer. If you have already committed your life to Jesus, use this prayer for renewal and praise.

Dear God, I come to you simply and honestly to confess that I have sinned, that sin is a part of who I am. And yet I know that you listen to sinners who are truthful before you. So I come with empty hands and heart, asking for forgiveness.

I confess that only through faith in Jesus Christ can I come to you. I confess my need for a Savior, and I thank you, Jesus, for dying on the cross to pay the price for my sins. Father, I ask that you forgive my sins and count me as righteous for Jesus' sake. Remove the guilt that accompanies my sin and bring me into your presence.

Holy Spirit of God, help me to pray, and teach me to live by your Word. Faithful God, help me to serve you faithfully. Make me more like Jesus each day, and help me to share with others the good news of your great salvation. In Jesus' name, Amen.

Bibliography

Barker, Kenneth L., and John R. Kohlenberger III. *Zondervan NIV Bible Commentary.* Grand Rapids, Mich.: Zondervan, 1994.

Boice, James M. *The Gospel of John.* Grand Rapids, Mich.: Baker, 2001.

Bowen, John P. *Evangelism for "Normal" People.* Minneapolis: Augsburg, 2002.

Bruce. F. F. *The Gospel of John.* Grand Rapids, Mich.: Eerdmans, 2004.

Carson, D. A. *The Gospel According to John.* Grand Rapids, Mich.: Eerdmans, 1991.

Guthrie, D., and J. A. Motyer, eds. *The New Bible Commentary: Revised.* Grand Rapids, Mich.: Eerdmans, 1970.

Morris, Leon. *The Gospel of John.* Grand Rapids, Mich.: Eerdmans, 1975.

NIV Serendipity Bible for Study Groups. Grand Rapids, Mich.: Zondervan, 1989.

NIV Study Bible. Grand Rapids, Mich.: Zondervan, 1985.

Ryan, Joseph. *That You May Believe.* Wheaton, Ill.: Crossway, 2003.

Strobel, Lee. *The Case for Christ.* Grand Rapids, Mich.: Zondervan, 1998.

Tasker, R. V. G. *The Gospel According to John.* Grand Rapids, Mich.: Eerdmans, 1971.

Yancey, Philip. *Where Is God When It Hurts?* Grand Rapids, Mich.: Zondervan, 1997.

Zacharias, Ravi. *Jesus Among Other Gods.* Nashville: Thomas Nelson, 2000.

Evaluation Questionnaire

DISCOVER JOHN: THE LAMB OF GOD

As you complete this study, please fill out this questionnaire to help us evaluate the effectiveness of our materials. Please be candid. Thank you.

1. Was this a home group ___ or a church-based ___ program? What church?

2. Was the study used for
   ___ a community evangelism group?
   ___ a community faith-nurture group?
   ___ a church Bible study group?

3. How would you rate the materials?

   Study Guide
   ___ excellent ___ very good ___ good ___ fair ___ poor

   Leader Guide
   ___ excellent ___ very good ___ good ___ fair ___ poor

4. What were the strengths?

5. What were the weaknesses?

6. What would you suggest to improve the material?

7. In general, what was the experience of your group?

Your name (optional) _____

Address _____

8. Other comments:

(Please fold, tape, stamp, and mail. Thank you.)

Faith Alive Christian Resources
2850 Kalamazoo Ave. SE
Grand Rapids, MI 49560